Time doesn't Exist

Time is a Convivence

Neelesh Kondaskar

pencil

ISBN 978-93-5458-771-9

Published in India 2021 by Pencil

A brand of
One Point Six Technologies Pvt. Ltd.
123, Building J2, Shram Seva Premises,
Wadala Truck Terminal, Wadala (E)
Mumbai 400037, Maharashtra, INDIA
E connect@thepencilapp.com
W www.thepencilapp.com

Author biography

The author is well versed in Science and Technology and depply intrested in astro physics.He is well versed with latest in astronomy and also on Artificial intelligence.
The Author has already published books on Artificail intelligence and on the Moon Missions.

CONTENTS

Introduction

We discuss the need of time in our life. Will our lives be better if there was no time? Does the high level of stress and anxiety in our life is because of time. What will be life like to live in a timeless society? Will there be disorder or life will be stress free. Will we have more freedom to do what we are interested? Is Time a scientific reality or scientific convenience we will dwell into it deeply? All this and more will be answered in this book.so start your journey.

Does Time Exist

Why is it that only Humans are conscious of time? Animals depend on the environment changes to decide to move from continents to continents. They follow the body signals to tell whether they are hungry or not .All the activities of animals follow a natural rhythm. Sleep Food, time of rest when to migrate to warmer or colder places it's the nature that decides for them. As the natural environment begins to change they decide to move on to the next place. They do not follow a clock or calendar to decide that it's time to move on. Many animals live together and do their hunting together. Do they watch the time and decide it's time to go for hunt.so even if they are living in large packs it's the environment that decides if it's time to hunt or stay. We humans are also social animals. There is not much that distinguishes us from animals. It's the ability to think which is much greater that distinguishes us from rest of the animals. So it's boon for us as well as a curse. We have made ourselves so much dependent on time that we have lost our natural touch .This natural touch is very essential for all including humans. Why do we humans have a fixed Lunch time, Dinner time snack Time. Is it that we have lost our natural instincts and are now dependent on the clock cycle? One may say that as we are conscious that's the reason time exists. Still can life come to an end if we stop watching the clock and depend on natural instincts? If we look at the universe level it's the change in the way matter interacts that results in weather a star is born or it remains as a floating gas. There is no universal clock which decides that after 1 billion years the star must collapse. Even if we just travel to other planets our definition of the 24 hour clock changes .So is it that time is manmade. It's made so that our life can become easier Humans have existed even when there was no mechanism to know the time. All our definition of time results from the Matter changing state weather we use atomic clocks or other means to measure it. We are always moving from a orderly state to a disorderly state. So it all started with Big bang where it was at the highest limit of order and it rate of disorder is only growing. So why do we need to add a time factor to all the events that are going from order to disorder. Is it that all the stars have to be born and die at only specific time scales? It's only the integration of matter that decides whether the star will burn fuel or explode. So why do we say that Time is the 4th Dimension. Does time really exists.

Time doesn't Exist

Time Slows or Speeds Up

A very big misconception is that Time slows if we travel at the speed of Light. Does time really slow or is it that Matter starts behaving differently as we move at faster speed. It's not the time that slows down but the rate of disorder that changes. The Sun travels around the Milkyway galaxy center at an incredible speed. We also travel along with the sun at the same speed. The sun speed varies depending on the point where it is from the center. Does it mean that time slows and speeds up with the speed of the sun. If that's so then why don't we adjust our clocks accordingly on a daily or yearly or monthly basis? After all the speed of travel is incredible either of the sun or the Earth moving around the sun in elliptical orbit.

So here again we have 2 motions which again complicates the idea of time slows as speed increases. So if we consider the entire solar system as one unit on which time is dependent we consider only the planet Earth as one unit which is moving around the Sun. If we increase the dimensions further the entire Milkyway galaxy is moving at a incredible speed so should we consider it and say time slows. So we cannot have one frame of speed to which we can pin our time with. So does time exists to slow. The atomic clocks measure time depending on the decay of matter considering the same matter on other planet where pressure ,temperature and other factors are different should we conclude that time slows or speeds up. Will the seasons of Summer Winter Rainy season get delayed or extended if time slows or moves Fast. It never does as Seasons don't depend on time but rather the position of the Earth with respect to the Sun. If the Earths speed changes the Duration of the seasons will change so why do we measure the Seasons in months and Days?

What is Reality of Time

We lead a stress full life just because we are in a Rat Race to be in time. We need everything on Time. So can we say time exists only for Human convenience? Will life as we know come to an end if the clocks stop ticking. Can life be simpler if instead of sequencing our tasks in reaction to time, we just leave it to completion of Task? Will life be less stressful? I surely think so. So will there be disorder in the society as we know of today. It surely will, but Humans thrived even when the time was not invented. So we will continue to thrive in a different life style which would be less stressful. If all things are done at a natural pace rather than a human defined time pace. We always have a quick lunch. Food needs to be chewed 32 times before slowing. That's natures pace. But today's lifestyle says Lunch is one hour so the Natural pace goes for a toss and we start the clock pace of eating food. As we go away from natural pace we swallow unthawed food which our natural digestive system cannot handle and we again fall sick with complains of digestion. As the clock ticks Anxiety and stress starts to develop to be within the hour to compete the Food.so we have less Focus and attention on our other tasks. This has a cascading effect on all the things in our daily life. So do we want time to rule over us? We need to ask ourselves. Materlistic society is designed around time. Will we starve to death if the Pizza is not delivered in 30 minutes. That's the question we need to ask. Why are we in such a hurry to be on time? All persons are made diffently.so their pace of work is different. When we put the boundaries of time we start to treat each person at same level and due to this cause stress and anxiety in the person.

Timeless Society

How will be a timeless society? .What will be life like in time less Society. It will be a society where humans will follow natural rhythm. As in urban life we wake up with alarm bells. It will be a place where people wake up naturally. They will work but the pace of work will be in sync with the natural rhythm. Work will be done without the stress of time. It may be delayed or might get done early but will being sync with Nature. Human needs have grown exponentially in the last 100 years and in the quest of satisfying those people spend more time acquiring them rather than enjoying them. To live in such a society we will need to lead a simple life in tune with the natural rhythm.

With Food shelter water and clean air being the priority. We still can find such life in remote villages so aren't they living and thriving? In the mad race with time humans have forgotten what they really need and are after things which don't add value to their life. We say we live in the age of information we often here the term information overload. Do we really need so much information that we cannot process or understand. So does it mean we will lead a primitive life? The answer is no? We still will do research and inventions which can help humankind progress but will be free from the bondage of time. Where work will not be deadlines but fulfilment of ones interests. People will work for the dreams without the pressure of doing it on time. So will there be no cooperative work done. It will be done but with understanding the human capability and natural pace of work. At this point we need to ask the basic question. Do we really need the modern gadgets which claim to make our life simpler or are these gadgets which are making us more deadline and time focused rather than life and nature focus?

Meditation and Time

When we become concisely aware of our body and surroundings we tend to reach a timeless state. There are saints and yogis who are in a meditative state for years together. They have the power to lower their metabolism and live for a longer period. So does the time as we know stop for them. What they are really doing is reducing the rate at which their body degrades. In meditative state the sense of time vanishes as we go deeper and deeper into the meditation. a study conducted on, participants reveals a interesting fact. The participants were asked to meditate in 2 intervals of 10 minutes each. In the second session of meditation, participants were asked to judge short and long intervals of time. Short intervals lasted between 15 seconds to 50 seconds and long intervals were between two to six minutes.

The study found that people who meditated underestimated short periods of time and overestimated long periods of time. Regardless of short or long time periods, people reported that they felt like time passed quickly during meditation compared to people who were not meditating. How our mind perceives time depends on a variety of factors, including the length of time being estimated. One theory is that we use mechanisms of our memory to recall how much time has passed. According to these memory-based models of how we judge time in short, our judgment of time depends on 1) how are we emotionally doing 2) How complex and how many events have happened 3) how demanding or how much attention the activity we do requires. The more a task requires of our attention, the more we tend to judge time to be longer and overestimate the passing of time. If you have driven a vehicle over long distances on an empty and straight highway, you may have experienced this fact. Moving a vehicle long distances in an area without traffic can start to make you feel less demanding of your attention, and you may find that several hours have passed even though it felt shorter. But if you are doing tasks that require a lot of attention, like driving in a crowded traffic jam, you may feel like a lot of time has passed even though it has only been a short while because you have had to do a lot more tasks and it has a been more mentally demanding of your attention. These results suggest that mindfulness meditation, a form of focused awareness, can be instrumental in how we perceive time. More broadly speaking, how we choose to engage with the world around us and how attentive we choose to be can deeply affect how we experience the passing of time day to day. If we are attentive and engaged moment to moment, with the same focus, awareness, and alertness that meditation demands, we may be able to experience a fuller and richer sense of the day—and it will, as a result, feel less like time moves fast. One can try a candle meditation, a version of a focused awareness meditation, and observe how meditation affects your perception of time. Light and/or place a candle about a foot in front of you, at or slightly below eye level. Find a comfortable seat with a tall spine, head reaching toward the ceiling. Set a timer for 7 minutes. Focus your eyes on the candle flame. Observe the flame for 7 minutes, closing your eyes when needed. Now that your mind has settled into the meditation, set your timer for 40 seconds. Observe the candle flame. At the end of the 40 seconds, observe: How did this short period of time feel to you? How long would you have estimated that length of time? Now set the timer now for 4 minutes. Observe the candle flame. At the end of the 3 minutes, observe: How did this short period of time feel to you? How long would you have estimated that length of time?

Notice if the shorter versus longer length of time felt different to you. So is it that our brain that decides what time it is. Again each person's experience is different so does time behave differently with each person.

Blackhole and Time

When a star of at least 20 solar mass reaches at its end of state, t explodes into a supernova. The core collapses under immense gravity and we get a Blackhole. So the Blackhole starts with the Matter that we are all aware of and then it crushes the matter under gravity that matter changes its state from what we know to the most fundamental nature of the particles.so does the collapse of the star and supernova explosion are time dependent or are they more of change of state of the matter. There is no rule that states that after 1million years the star should explode in supernova and after that it should turn into a Blackhole.

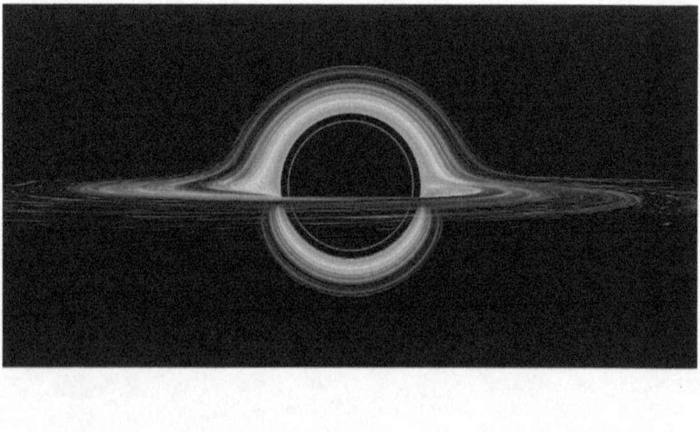

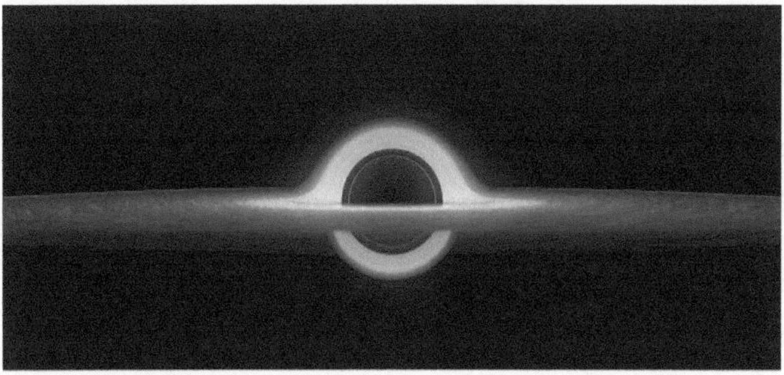

It's the process of conversion of Hydrogen to helium and ultimately to Iron that makes the change does time come into picture. Matter as we know behaves vierdly as we approach Blackholes. Balckholes are known for their immense gravitational pull which does not even allow the light to go past it .As we approach a Blabckhole the matter as we know starts to disintegrate into more and more of its fundamental particles .Here all the laws of physics as applicable on Earth fail as we approach nearer to the Blackhole. So is it that the Time changes or the the matter that changes its state. From the known states of matter in which we live matter disintegrates into its fundamental particles. Matter behaves more vierdly as we approach Balckholes so we can say that any object will change its state. So does this mean that time slows down or comes to a halt or is it that the laws governing the states of matter change. It's more of the latter than Time changing its rate. Matter behaves in such a fashion that is still a subject of study. We have not yet gone close enough to a Blackhole yet to understand its true nature. Whatever conclusions that we may draw that may change as we study the Blackholes more closely with better instruments.

Time and Conciseness

Does conciseness create time? Do we need time to make complete tasks? If we look at the subconscious level most of the actions are run independent of time. The beating of the heart or flow of blood in the veins it does not depend on time. But our conscious actions are always time dependent. Deadlines to meet tasks to be completed on time determine weather we are successful or unsuccessful as a person. So time is more of a convince tool to live a materialistic lifestyle. The present materialistic lifestyle will not be possible without time. With our consciousness we can create our reality and today we humans are more bent towards material pursuits which requires a clock to tick. What humanity has achieved in past 200 years would not have been possible without having time to sequence our events.

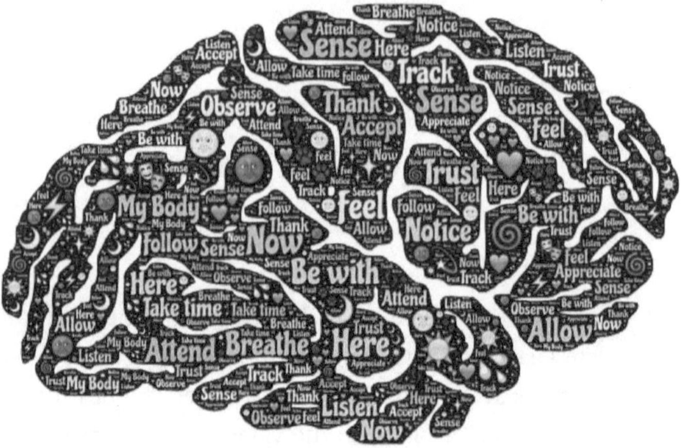

But as we make advances in Technology we realize that materialistic living is not the right way to live. We now have a strong awareness and tendency to go back to Nature and live among the Nature. Which again raises the question do we require time. As we race to colonize different Planets in the Solar System measuring time will play an important role in getting us there but will time be required beyond that. As all humans have the urge to move out of the rat race time is the most important factor leading to the stress. We should restrict time only to sequence events and we should not make it a part of our life where time dictates all our needs. We should not resist Technology development but we must also ensure that life as we know is in tune with the natural rhythms. This can only be realized when we become consciously aware of our surroundings and live a life in tune with that. Instead of going with the clock we must move with what our body life and nature demands.

Reality and Consciousness

What is reality? Does reality vary from person to person? Does a blind man experience the same reality that a normal person does? The answer lies in the way the brain process the information. The brain depends on our sensory inputs to create a picture. The sensory inputs are vision, hearing, taste, smell. Based on these inputs and the memory that's stores we create our reality. This reality varies from person to person.so if any of the sensory information is not present example vision the brain compensates it by making other senses stronger. So reality is just an illusion. So this illusionary reality require time to exist absolutely not. As Time is not one of the sensory inputs to the brain. Again if we see the light spectrum or the sound frequencies we only can sense a minute part of the spectrum .

So if we see the reality we create is just based on the way a minute information is processed. A dog has a better sense of smell so his world will be filled more from the aromas of nature rather than the vision. So then where does time come into picture? The life nowadays has become more of task oriented rather than nature oriented. So in today's world success is measured by the number of tasks completed rather than living in tune with nature. Just 25 years ago mobile did not exist but still life was going on smoothly and today we cannot think of life without mobile. So with the increase of devices and materialism in life to manage these we require time. If we remove all the modern clutter will we still require time? Our bodies still are dependent on natural cycles rather than on time cycles. The body rhythm is in sync with daylight and night. The body does not depend on 24 hour atomic clock to sequence its events rather even today it depends on the day and night for sequencing the body functioning. Does it mean that we remove technology and innovation from life? Absolutely not rather let's build technology to be in tune with nature and help us survive the natural calamities. We today are going on a path where we getting more technology dependent for survival rather than the other way round. So being consciously aware of the surroundings and living according with the tune of nature is true living what do say?

Planets and Time

The 24 hour clock cycle that we use on Earth to measure time will be menigless if we just move out of Earth.Our 24 hours depends on the one complete revolution
of the Earth around its own axis.So if we consider different planets and we use Earths 24 hours as criteria ,time will vary considerably on different panets.So the time we use can only be strictly used on Earth.Below is the variation in time.

Planet	**Rotation Period Time**	**Revolution Period**
Mercury	58.6 days	87.97 days
Venus	243 days	224.7 days
Earth	0.99 days	365.26 days
Mars	1.03 days	1.88 years
Jupiter	0.41 days	11.86 years
Saturn	0.45 days	29.46 years
Uranus	0.72 days	84.01 years
Neptune	0.67 days	164.79

years
Pluto 6.39 days
248.59 years

So our 40 hour work week will vary completely on diffrent planets.So here again we see that time is just aconvience tool built on all the Earth Parameter.We move out of Earth things change.

Who decides

The present times in the materialistic world are dominated by lot of information. Our lifestyle is completely overwhelmed by this information overload. We are constantly bombarded by thousands of advertisements driving us in different direction. In today's age we tend to buy a lot of things which we really don't require. So the question arises are we the ones deciding for ourselves. The advertisements nowadays are emotional and also visually appealing so we may tend to buy a sports car running at 250 km/hour but there will be no road for it drive on.So the materialistic world depends on consumption. The more the consumption the better. In the race able to afford things we tend to have a race with our 24 hour clock. We tend to believe that we need to do more in the 24 hours we have to buy that object.

What we tend to forget that in the process to over achieve in the 24 hours our human body takes a toll as its is not used to this rhythm. We tend to go against the natural rhythm to achieve more in the 24 hours. So we compromise on sleep, we tend to eat fast and a lot more abuses to our body. The end result we fall sick. As our belief system is we have limited amount of time. A time which is nonexistent. So if we manage to decide independently what we want without the influence of advertisers we will have less needs to satisfy and we will have a healthy mind and body. The stress levels will also come down and if we go by our general perception we will have more time. So is it the right moment to decide on our own what we really want and live life on our terms. Or do we want to have a life of endless needs for which we go against our natural rhythm to achieve and lead a stress and life of illness and at the end we blame everything on time. We go to at great lengths in blaming time by using my time is bad, not the right time and so on .whereas the fault lies within and not on time.

Spirituality Today

What is spirituality? What do we understand when we say spiritual living. Is it abandoning all and living life discretely. Even though there may be different understandings of spiritual living the one we interpret here is living life being consciously aware of one self. A meditative life. Does Time Exist at Spiritual Level? When a person rises at spiritual level the concept of time disappears. We tend to transcend into a different kind of reality.

Do such persons exist yeah, they do. So when we take it not from technology level but at spiritual level here also time is not required. There are many paths to attain spiritual level and the same has been achieved by many. So here the reality as they perceive changes. So is this life better or not that will be a personnel decision. To live a materlist life or to live a spiritual and nature tuned life. We still are very far away with our present technology to mimic spiritual life technologically. But then it's not the only path. So a day may come when we realize this reality technologically, till that time it will be only for the select few people who tend to choose to live life differently will experience it. These people are in minority and for all of us we will have to wait till we technologically advance enough to see it.

Theory of Relativity and Time

Is time a universal measurement? Does it vary? Today our lives are governed by the seconds, minutes, hours, days, and weeks, regardless of where we live on the globe, time will never be absolute. The rate at which it passes depends completely on your velocity and acceleration at any given instant. But can time be slower and faster at the same time? The rate at which time passes actually slows down the more you're moving as compared to a stationary object. Our perception of time, suggests it is actually speeding up, thanks to the technology advance we have today here we talk about rate of actual time, shown in numerous experiments to slow down when particles such as muons and photons speed up In

Einstein's theory of relativity, time dilation describes a

difference of elapsed time between two events, as measured by observers that are either moving relative to each other, or differently, depending on their proximity to a gravitational mass. Basically, it states that the faster we go, the more the time is affected. But if time is as relative as this suggests, it can seem a little contradictory. Imagine if me and my friend are in two different spacecraft's. They are moving in space in opposite direction. Suppose if suddenly they cross by each other (change directions). From my perspective it seems like my friends moving, and so time should go more slowly for him, but from my friends perspective, it seems like I'm moving, so it should go more slowly for me. So how can we both think time is going more slowly for the other person? Someone's time must actually be slower, right? Well, no, sorry. We wish it were that simple. The explanation has to do with how you rotate the direction of time itself every time you change speeds. So here again we conclude that time is just for our convenience as it totally depends on the state of the observer and the objects motion relative to it. If we replace time by degradation of an object as speed increases or decreases it will give a better understanding.

Quantum Time

As has been proven with experiments if we split a photon and move them away from each other. One type of action on one part of photon the same is seen on the other instantaneously. Here actions take place simultaneously rather than at a different time. So at quantum level there is no time governing the actions. Quantum world is weirder where any particle can exist at any place at any given instant. So when an observer tries to measure the action its randomness collapses. So here also all events are action driven rather than Time driven.

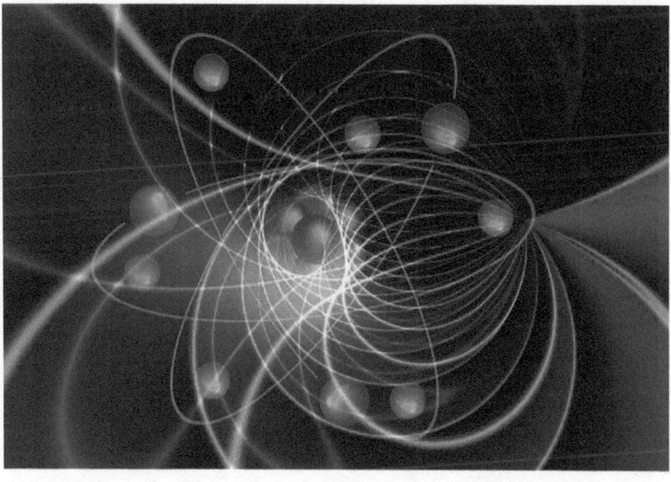

So the way we see reality at our level is completely different at the quantum level. So here there is no concept of being somewhere here it is being present everywhere at the same time. These behaviors tend to collapse as we go on dealing with atom and molecular level. The type of matter which we are made up of and we interact with. So if we drill down to the basic level the concept of time is completely absent and as we move up the ladder we feel the need of it for our convenience. Here there is no concept of past present and future which is man made for his own convenience. Here everything exists simultaneously. We are all made up of quantum particles which are clubbed together to form what we are .All our laws of physics, chemistry are derived from the behavior of this group under certain conditions. You just change one condition and the Physics changes. Like Matter behaviors completely differently when we increase the pressure. Just a common example we can boil water fast if we more pressure is applied. So it's more of our own limitations of our understanding that makes us believe that Time exists whereas at Quantum level all our know concepts go bust. We need a different level of understanding to grasp it.

Past Present and Future

We only define past present and future as we believe in time. If we remove time there will be no past present and future .As we are advancing in technology we now come to the concept that past present and future exist simultaneously. If so then why is time required. We presently are restricted to only 3 Dimensions. If we move up the ladder in dimensions maybe we can understand it better and will be able to live anywhere simultaneously. This also brings another concept of Multiverse where our actions can give rise to another universe in which we tend to peruse the action and in other universe we peruse a different action. We need to raise our technology barrier higher enough to completely understand the concept. As the telescopes become more and more sensitive we are able to go back to events which have taken place in the past. So do we say past exists? Past also is effectively captured by our brain and we form memories.

These memories shape our present. So can we say that past and present exist? Simultaneously. So what about Future. There are astrologers and Physic who can see Future. If we believe in them they are seeing the Future then Future already exists otherwise they cannot see it or feel it. Does it mean that our limitations as Humans we cannot see it means that it does not exist? So either astrologers or Physic are wrong or it's that Future already exits. In the same length when we say information will always exist so why not the past present future of an object be present simultaneously. Are we limited to the accessibility of the information that we tend to believe that past of an object does not exist or future does not exist. As information defines how an object appears in our reality. If we look at in terms of cosmic scale whatever supernova explosions or stars we are observing, we are seeing them as they appeared in the past. So the information exists in form of gravitational waves, Visible light, rays form and could be in many other forms which we so far have not been able to decipher. So information of past exists. So on a similar scale future must also exist. So the concept of past time, Present time and future time is meaningless. We are only limited by our technology advances. As we progress technically we will tend to appreciate the fact .So here again we do not require time or the universe is not time dependent for its events.

Conclusion

We live in a society where dominant thoughts influence the masses. We have been so entrenched in time that we now believe that life is not possible without time. We have enslaved ourselves to time so much that our health and wellbeing is also at stake. The rate at which we are moving will one day break us. Is it not worthy to go back to the natural rhythm of life .I leave it to you to decide?